ARLO HOME SECURITY SYSTEM USER GUIDE

Troubleshooting Tips, Installation Instructions, Smart Security Integration, and Related Set up Guide for Arlo Security

By

Roy Murray

Copyright © 2024 Roy Murray,

Table of Contents

Introduction

The Arlo Home Security System is an exceptional choice for anyone seeking a reliable and user-friendly security solution. From the moment you unbox it, the attention to detail and quality is evident. Setting up the system is as easy as anything you can think of, thanks to the intuitive app and clear instructions. The cameras offer crystal-clear video quality, even at night, and the motion detection feature is highly sensitive and customizable.

One of the standout features is the seamless integration with other smart home devices, allowing you to control everything from your phone or voice assistant. The two-way audio is a great touch, making it easy to communicate with visitors or deter intruders. Plus, the system's sleek design blends in well with any home décor.

The subscription plans are reasonably priced and offer excellent value, with advanced features like person detection and cloud storage. Overall, the Arlo Home Security System is a top-notch choice that delivers peace of mind and security, all wrapped up in a sleek and modern package. Highly recommended for anyone looking to enhance their home security!

I decided to write this user guide for the Arlo Home Security System because I recognized the need for a comprehensive resource that caters to both new and experienced users. Security technology is continually evolving, and while Arlo offers robust features, the full potential of these systems can only be realized with a clear understanding of their capabilities and setup.

For new customers, navigating the initial setup and understanding the various features can be overwhelming. This guide aims to simplify that process, offering step-by-step instructions and tips to get the system up and running smoothly. It's about helping new users feel confident and secure from the start.

For existing customers, this guide serves as a valuable resource for exploring advanced features and integrating their system with other smart home devices. Whether it's optimizing camera placement, customizing notifications, or utilizing the latest updates, I wanted to provide a resource that helps users make the most of their investment.

Ultimately, this guide is about empowering users- new and old alike- to fully leverage the Arlo Home Security System, ensuring they can protect their homes and loved ones with confidence and ease.

Benefits of using Arlo systems

The Arlo Security System offers a range of benefits that make it an attractive choice for homeowners looking to enhance their security. Here are some key advantages:

1. **High-Quality Video and Audio**: Arlo cameras provide high-definition video quality, ensuring clear and detailed footage, even in low-light conditions. The system also includes two-way audio, allowing users to communicate with visitors or potential intruders.
2. **Wireless and Flexible Installation**: Arlo systems are known for their wireless design, which makes installation easy and flexible. You can place cameras almost anywhere, both indoors and outdoors, without the hassle of running wires.
3. **Advanced Motion Detection**: The system's motion detection capabilities are highly customizable, allowing users to set specific zones and sensitivity levels. This helps reduce false alarms and ensures that you are alerted to real threats.

4. **Smart Home Integration**: Arlo integrates seamlessly with other smart home systems, including Amazon Alexa, Google Assistant, and Apple HomeKit. This enables voice control and allows users to incorporate Arlo into a broader smart home ecosystem.
5. **Remote Access and Control**: With the Arlo app, users can access live video feeds, recorded footage, and system settings from anywhere. This remote access provides peace of mind and allows for quick responses to any incidents.
6. **Cloud and Local Storage Options**: Arlo offers both cloud storage and local storage options, providing flexibility in how you store and access your footage. Cloud storage plans come with added features like advanced detection and activity zones.
7. **Scalability and Customization**: Whether you need a basic setup with just a few cameras or a more comprehensive system with multiple devices, Arlo offers scalable options to suit different needs and budgets. The system's features can be tailored to your specific security requirements.
8. **Durability and Weather Resistance**: Arlo cameras are designed to withstand various weather conditions, making them suitable for outdoor use. This durability ensures reliable performance year-round.

Overall, the Arlo Home Security System combines ease of use, advanced features, and integration capabilities, making it a versatile and effective solution for safeguarding your home and family.

General Safety Information for Arlo Home Security System

- **Electrical Safety:** Ensure that all Arlo devices, including cameras and base stations, are connected to the appropriate power sources and voltage levels. Avoid overloading electrical outlets and use surge protectors if necessary.
- **Battery Safety:** Only use the batteries and chargers specified by Arlo for your devices. Do not attempt to disassemble or modify the batteries. Dispose of used batteries in accordance with local regulations.
- **Water and Moisture:** While Arlo cameras are designed to be weather-resistant, avoid submerging them in water or exposing them to excessive moisture. Install cameras in locations where they are protected from direct water exposure.

- **Heat and Ventilation:** Do not place Arlo devices near heat sources, such as radiators, stoves, or other appliances that produce heat. Ensure adequate ventilation around the devices to prevent overheating.

- **Secure Mounting:** Use the provided mounting hardware to install Arlo cameras securely. Ensure that the mounting surface can support the weight of the camera and that the installation is stable and secure.
- **Height and Accessibility:** Install cameras at a height that is out of reach of unauthorized individuals but accessible for maintenance and battery replacement. Use caution when using ladders or other tools during installation.
- **Cable Management:** Keep cables organized and secured to prevent tripping hazards. Avoid running cables through areas with high foot traffic or where they may be easily damaged.

- **Respecting Privacy:** When installing cameras, be mindful of privacy laws and regulations in your area. Position cameras to avoid capturing footage of areas where individuals may have a reasonable expectation of privacy, such as bathrooms, bedrooms, or neighbouring properties.
- **Data Security:** Use strong, unique passwords for your Arlo account and enable two-factor authentication to protect your account from unauthorized access. Regularly update your devices and the Arlo app to the latest software versions for enhanced security.

- **Cleaning:** Clean Arlo devices with a soft, dry cloth. Do not use harsh chemicals, solvents, or abrasive materials that could damage the equipment.
- **Firmware Updates:** Regularly check for firmware updates for your Arlo devices. Firmware updates often include important security patches and feature enhancements.

- **Compliance:** Ensure that your use of the Arlo Home Security System complies with local laws and regulations regarding surveillance and recording. This includes obtaining consent from individuals if required by law.
- **Interference:** Arlo devices operate on specific frequencies and should not interfere with other electronic devices. If you experience

interference, consult the user manual or contact Arlo support for assistance.

- **Emergency Situations:** The Arlo Home Security System is designed to enhance security but should not be relied upon as the sole means of emergency detection or response. In case of an emergency, contact local authorities immediately.
- **Customer Support:** For assistance with installation, troubleshooting, or other issues, contact Arlo customer support or refer to the Arlo website for resources and support options.

Chapter 1: Getting Started
Unboxing Your Arlo System

Upon receiving your Arlo Home Security System, you should find the following components neatly packed in the box. Carefully remove each item and ensure all components are included and undamaged. Keep the packaging materials for future use or warranty purposes.

List of Included Components

1. **Arlo Cameras**

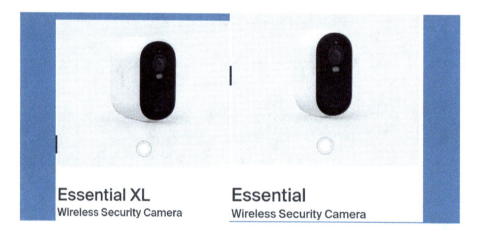

Essential XL
Wireless Security Camera

Essential
Wireless Security Camera

- o The kit you purchased may include one or more cameras. Each camera will have a protective cover and may come with additional accessories.
2. **Base Station or SmartHub**

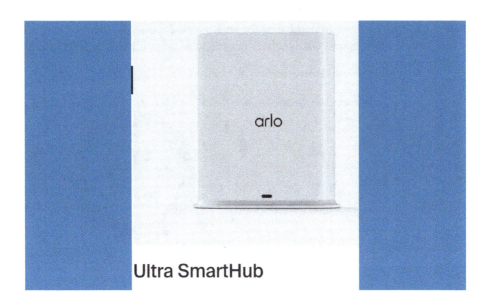

Ultra SmartHub

This is the central unit that connects your cameras to your home network. It may have a power adapter, an Ethernet cable, and possibly a USB drive for local storage.

3. **Mounting Hardware**

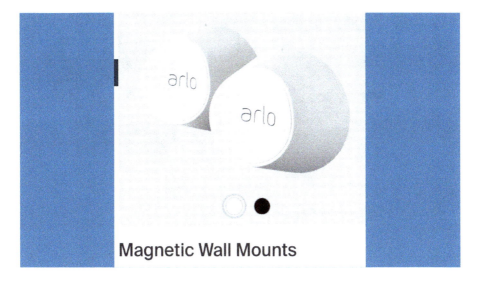

Magnetic Wall Mounts

Wall mounts, screws, and anchors for securing the cameras to walls or other surfaces. Some kits may also include magnetic mounts for easy repositioning.

4. **Rechargeable Batteries**

Go 1 Rechargeable Battery   **8 ft. Indoor Magnetic Charging...**

Batteries for each camera, along with a charger or power adapter. Some kits may include additional spare batteries or a charging station.

5. **Power Adapters and Cables**

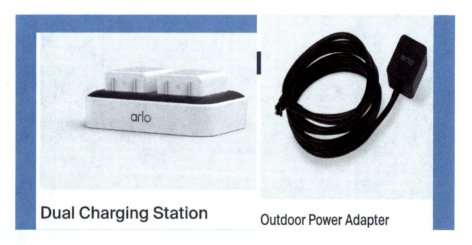

Dual Charging Station   Outdoor Power Adapter

Power adapters for the cameras and base station, along with any necessary USB or charging cables.

6. **Quick Start Guide**

A printed guide providing initial setup instructions and basic information about the system.

7. **Warranty and Safety Information**

Documents detailing the warranty coverage and safety precautions.

8. **Optional Accessories (if included)**

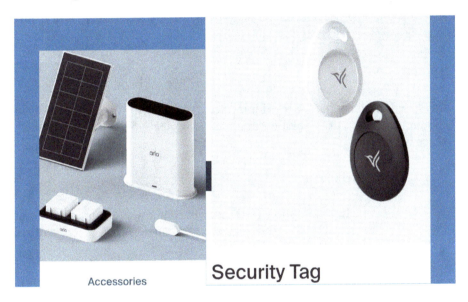

Accessories

Security Tag

This could include items like outdoor security mounts, additional battery packs, or solar panels for continuous charging.

Checking the Package Contents

Before proceeding with the setup, take a moment to verify that all components listed above are present. If any items are missing or appear damaged, contact Arlo customer support or the retailer from whom you purchased the system.

Handling and Storage of Components

- **Handle with Care:** While Arlo components are designed to be durable, handle them with care, especially the cameras and lenses. Avoid touching the lens with your fingers to prevent smudges or damage.
- **Keep in a Safe Place:** Store any unused accessories or documentation in a safe, easily accessible location. This will be useful for future reference or if you need to reinstall the system.

With all components accounted for, you are ready to proceed with the installation and setup of your Arlo Home Security System. Ensure that you have a stable internet connection and any necessary tools, such as a drill or screwdriver, for mounting the cameras.

System Overview

As stated earlier, the Arlo Home Security System is a versatile and comprehensive security solution designed to protect your home and provide peace of mind.

Key Features include:

- High-definition (HD) and ultra-high-definition (4K) video resolution, ensuring clear and detailed footage both day and night.
- A wireless design, making installation straightforward and flexible. This allows for easy relocation and adjustment of cameras as needed.
- Infrared night vision- Arlo cameras can capture clear footage in low-light conditions, enhancing security during nighttime hours.
- Built-in microphones and speakers, enable two-way communication. This feature is useful for interacting with visitors or deterring potential intruders.
- Advanced motion detection technology allows for customizable detection zones and sensitivity settings, minimizing false alarms and focusing on critical areas.
- Flexible storage solutions, including cloud storage plans for secure access to your footage from anywhere. Additionally,

some models support local storage through USB drives or microSD cards.

o Compatible with major smart home platforms, including Amazon Alexa, Google Assistant, and Apple HomeKit. This integration allows for voice control and automation within a broader smart home ecosystem.

o Remote access to your system, enabling live streaming, video playback, and system management from your smartphone or tablet.

o Instant alerts and notifications are based on specific events, such as motion detection or sound activation. Customize the alert settings to suit your preferences and needs.

o Designed to withstand various weather conditions, making them suitable for both indoor and outdoor use.

Understanding the Different Models and Configurations

Arlo offers a range of camera models and configurations to suit different security needs:

1. **Arlo Pro Series**

Pro 5S 2K
Wireless Security Camera

Known for its advanced features, the Arlo Pro series offers high-resolution video, rechargeable batteries, and smart features like activity zones and person detection.

2. **Arlo Ultra Series**

Ultra 2
Wireless Security Camera

The Ultra series provides 4K video resolution, enhanced night vision, and a wider field of view. It's ideal for those seeking the highest quality footage and advanced security features.

3. **Arlo Essential Series**

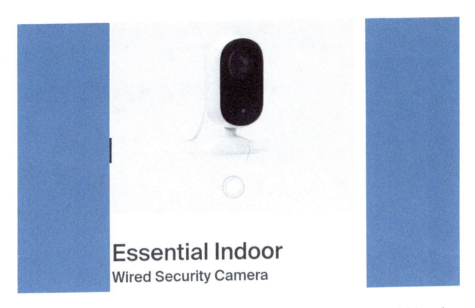

Essential Indoor
Wired Security Camera

The Essential series offers core security features at a more affordable price point. These cameras are easy to install and maintain, making them a great choice for basic home security.

4. **Arlo Floodlight and Doorbell Cameras**

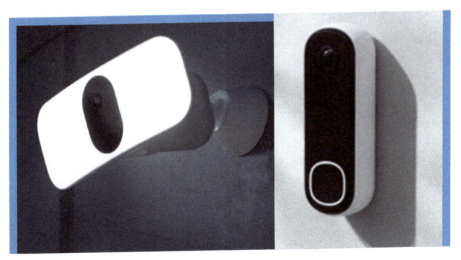

These specialized cameras provide additional functionality, such as floodlighting and doorbell integration, for enhanced outdoor security and visitor management.

Wire-Free Keypad

Go 2
LTE/Wi-Fi Security Camera

5. **Arlo Baby and Arlo Q Series**

These models are designed for indoor use, with features like two-way audio, temperature monitoring, and advanced video analytics.

Choosing the Right Configuration

When selecting an Arlo system, consider factors such as the size of your property, specific security needs (e.g., outdoor monitoring, baby monitoring), and your budget. Arlo's modular design allows you to expand your system over time, adding additional cameras and accessories as needed.

Setting Up Your Arlo System

Setting up your Arlo Security System is a straightforward process that involves creating an account, installing the hardware, and configuring the system to meet your needs. Follow these steps to ensure a smooth and efficient setup.

Creating an Arlo Account

To get started, you'll need to create an Arlo account. This account allows you to manage your devices, access your footage, and customize your system's settings.

Download the Arlo App: Available for both iOS and Android devices, the Arlo app is essential for setting up and managing your system. Download it from the App Store or Google Play Store.

Sign Up or Log In: Open the Arlo app and select "Sign Up" to create a new account. If you already have an Arlo account, simply log in with your credentials.

Verify Your Email: After signing up, you'll receive an email verification link. Click the link to verify your email address and activate your account.

Installing the Arlo Base Station or SmartHub

The base station or SmartHub is the central unit that connects your cameras to your home network. It also serves as a hub for local storage if supported.

Connect to Power and Internet: Plug the base station into a power outlet using the provided power adapter. Connect the base station to your router using the Ethernet cable included in the package.

Power On: Turn on the base station and wait for the power and internet LED indicators to turn solid green, indicating a successful connection.

Sync the Base Station: Follow the prompts in the Arlo app to sync the base station with your account. This process usually involves pressing a sync button on the base station.

Setting Up and Positioning Your Cameras

Proper camera placement is crucial for optimal coverage and performance.

Charge or Install Batteries: Insert the provided batteries into each camera, or connect them to power using the included adapters. Make sure the batteries are fully charged before mounting the cameras.

Sync Cameras with the Base Station: Press the sync button on the base station, then press the sync button on the camera. The camera's LED should blink blue, indicating it is syncing with the base station. Repeat this process for each camera.

Choose Installation Locations: Position cameras at entry points, such as doors and windows, and in areas requiring monitoring, like the living room or backyard. Ensure cameras are installed at a height that balances coverage and accessibility.

Mount the Cameras: Use the provided mounting hardware to secure the cameras to walls or other surfaces. For outdoor cameras, make sure they are protected from the elements but still have a clear view.

Configuring Your System in the Arlo App

Once the hardware is set up, use the Arlo app to configure your system settings.

Name Your Devices: Assign names to each camera for easy identification (e.g., "Front Door," "Backyard").

Set Up Motion Detection Zones: Customize motion detection zones and sensitivity levels to focus on specific areas and reduce false alarms.

Wire-Free Outdoor Siren

Configure Alerts and Notifications: Choose how and when to receive notifications for motion or sound events. Options include push notifications, email alerts, and more.

Enable Two-Way Audio: If your cameras support two-way audio, enable this feature to communicate with visitors or intruders through the app.

Finalizing Setup and Testing

After completing the setup, test your system to ensure everything is working correctly.

Check Live Feeds: View the live feed from each camera through the Arlo app to confirm proper positioning and functionality.

Test Motion Detection: Trigger the motion sensors to verify that alerts are being sent correctly and that the camera captures the necessary footage.

Adjust Settings as Needed: Fine-tune settings for video quality, recording duration, and other preferences to optimize your system's performance.

Positioning Your Arlo Cameras

Proper placement of your Arlo cameras is crucial for maximizing the effectiveness of your home security system. Good positioning ensures optimal coverage, clear footage, and reliable detection of events. Here are some guidelines and best practices for positioning your Arlo cameras:

1. Key Areas to Monitor

Identify the critical areas around your property that you want to monitor. Common locations include:

- **Entry Points:** Doors, windows, and gates are prime locations for cameras, as these are common entry points for intruders.
- **Driveways and Garages:** Monitoring these areas helps keep an eye on vehicles and anyone approaching your home.
- **Yards and Gardens:** Cameras positioned here can capture movement around the perimeter of your property.

- **Indoor Spaces:** Consider placing cameras in high-traffic areas inside your home, such as hallways, living rooms, and staircases.

2. Height and Angle

The height and angle of your camera placement significantly impact the quality and effectiveness of the footage.

- **Optimal Height:** Place cameras at a height of 7-10 feet (2-3 meters) off the ground. This height is high enough to avoid tampering but low enough to capture clear details.
- **Angling the Camera:** Tilt the camera slightly downward for a better view of faces and activities. This angle also helps reduce the range of the camera's motion detection, focusing it on relevant areas.
- **Avoiding Glare:** Position cameras to avoid direct sunlight or bright lights, which can cause glare and affect video quality. If placing cameras outdoors, consider shaded areas or use camera hoods.

3. Coverage and Field of View

Consider the camera's field of view (FOV) to ensure comprehensive coverage of the area.

- **Wide-Angle Coverage:** Arlo cameras typically offer wide-angle lenses, ranging from 110° to 180° FOV. Position the camera to maximize coverage while minimizing blind spots.
- **Overlap Coverage:** If using multiple cameras, overlap their fields of view slightly to ensure seamless coverage of your property without gaps.

4. Weather and Environmental Considerations

Outdoor cameras must withstand various weather conditions.

- **Weather Resistance:** Arlo cameras are designed to be weather-resistant, but it's still best to place them in sheltered areas to protect them from direct exposure to rain, snow, and extreme temperatures.

- **Stable Mounting:** Ensure the cameras are securely mounted to withstand wind and other environmental factors.

5. Privacy and Legal Considerations

When positioning your cameras, respect the privacy of others and comply with local laws.

- **Private Areas:** Avoid positioning cameras in a way that invades the privacy of others, such as pointing them into neighbours' yards, windows, or bathrooms.
- **Public and Shared Spaces:** Be mindful of cameras capturing footage in shared or public spaces, and ensure compliance with local surveillance laws.

6. Accessibility for Maintenance

Position cameras where they are accessible for regular maintenance, such as cleaning the lenses and changing batteries.

- **Battery Access:** If using battery-powered cameras, place them where you can easily access them for recharging or replacing batteries.
- **Cleaning:** Ensure that the cameras can be reached for occasional cleaning to maintain clear footage.

7. Testing and Adjustment

After positioning your cameras, use the Arlo app to test the coverage and adjust the placement as needed.

- **Live View Testing:** Check the live feed to confirm that the camera captures the desired areas and that the image quality is satisfactory.
- **Motion Detection Testing:** Test the motion detection settings to ensure that the cameras alert you to relevant activities without excessive false alarms.

Connecting Your Devices

Connecting your Arlo devices, including cameras, base stations, and other accessories, is a crucial step in setting up your home security system. Follow these steps to ensure a smooth and successful connection process.

Connecting the Base Station or SmartHub

The base station or SmartHub serves as the central hub for your Arlo system, connecting your cameras to the internet and managing communications.

- **Power Up the Base Station:**
  - o Connect the base station to a power outlet using the provided power adapter. Wait for the power LED to turn green, indicating the device is powered on.
- **Connect to the Internet:**
  - o Use the Ethernet cable included in your package to connect the base station to your home router. The internet LED on the base station should turn green once connected.
- **Sync with the Arlo App:**
  - o Open the Arlo app and log into your account. Follow the on-screen instructions to add the base station to your system. This may involve scanning a QR code or entering a device ID.

Connecting Arlo Cameras

After setting up the base station, it's time to connect your cameras.

- **Power the Cameras:**
  - o Insert the provided batteries into each camera or connect them to power using the included adapters. For rechargeable batteries, ensure they are fully charged.
- **Position Cameras for Syncing:**
  - o Place the cameras close to the base station for initial syncing. This helps ensure a strong connection during the setup process.
- **Sync Cameras with the Base Station:**
  - o Press the sync button on the base station. The sync LED will blink, indicating the base station is in sync mode.

o   On each camera, press the sync button. The camera's LED should blink blue, signalling it is syncing with the base station. Once the LED turns solid blue, the camera is successfully connected.

- **Verify Connection:**
  o   Check the Arlo app to ensure each camera is displayed and connected. You should be able to view live feeds and adjust settings for each camera.

Adding Additional Devices and Accessories

If your system includes additional devices, such as doorbells, lights, or other sensors, follow these steps:

- **Doorbells and Chimes:**

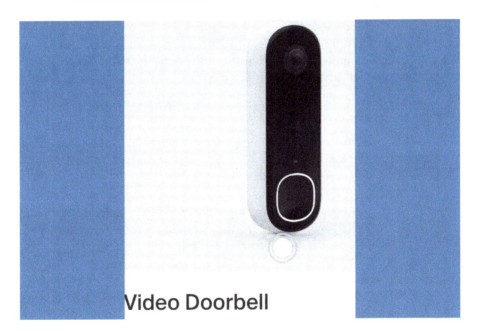

Video Doorbell

If you have an Arlo doorbell, connect it to your system by following the specific instructions provided with the device. This usually involves syncing the doorbell with the base station and setting up notifications.

- **Lights and Other Sensors:**

Arlo Pro 3 Floodlight Camera

For Arlo lights or other sensors, ensure they are powered on and follow the syncing process similar to the cameras. Use the Arlo app to add these devices to your system and customize their settings.

Configuring Your Network and System Settings

Once all devices are connected, configure your network and system settings for optimal performance.

- **Wi-Fi Settings:**
  - If your cameras support a direct Wi-Fi connection (without a base station), ensure they are connected to a stable Wi-Fi network. Enter your Wi-Fi credentials through the Arlo app during setup.
- **Network Security:**
  - Use strong, unique passwords for your Wi-Fi network and Arlo account to protect against unauthorized access. Enable two-factor authentication for added security.
- **Firmware Updates:**
  - Check for any firmware updates for your Arlo devices. Keeping your system updated ensures you have the latest features and security enhancements.

After all devices are connected and configured, perform a thorough test to ensure everything is functioning correctly.

- o View the live feed from each camera through the Arlo app to confirm proper placement and functionality.
- o Test the motion detection and alert system by walking in front of each camera. Check that you receive notifications and that the cameras record the events properly.
- o If your Arlo system is integrated with other smart home devices (like lights, locks, or voice assistants), test the integration to ensure smooth operation.

Chapter 2: Using the Arlo App

Navigating the Arlo App

The Arlo app is a central tool for managing and controlling your Arlo Home Security System. It provides access to live feeds, system settings, and notifications, allowing you to monitor and customize your security setup from anywhere. Here's what to do to navigate the Arlo app effectively.

1. Getting Started with the Arlo App

- **Download and Install:**
  - Download the Arlo app from the App Store (iOS) or Google Play Store (Android). Install the app on your smartphone or tablet.
- **Log In:**
  - Open the app and log in using your Arlo account credentials. If you don't have an account, follow the prompts to create one.

2. Home Screen Overview

- **Dashboard:**
  - The home screen displays an overview of your connected devices. You'll see a list of your cameras and other Arlo devices with their current status (online/offline).
- **Live Feed:**
  - Tap on a device to view its live video feed. This screen shows real-time footage and allows you to interact with the camera's features, such as two-way audio and video recording.

3. Accessing Camera Feeds

- **View Live Feed:**
  - From the home screen, select a camera to view its live feed. You can swipe to view other cameras or use the "Live View" option to check multiple feeds simultaneously.
- **Playback Recorded Footage:**

- To view recorded footage, navigate to the "Library" tab. Here, you can access video clips saved to the cloud or local storage.
- **Zoom and Pan:**
  - Use pinch-to-zoom gestures to zoom in on the live feed or recorded footage. Pan the view by dragging your finger across the screen.

4. Configuring Device Settings

- **Access Device Settings:**
  - Tap on the gear icon or the camera's name to access its settings. Here you can adjust various parameters, including video quality, motion detection zones, and alert settings.
- **Customize Motion Detection:**
  - Set up and modify motion detection zones and sensitivity levels to tailor the camera's alert system to your needs.
- **Enable/Disable Features:**
  - Turn on or off features such as two-way audio, night vision, and activity zones. You can also configure recording schedules and adjust alert preferences.

5. Managing Notifications and Alerts

- **Set Up Alerts:**
  - Go to the "Settings" menu and select "Notifications" to customize how and when you receive alerts. Options include push notifications, email alerts, and more.
- **View Alert History:**
  - Access your alert history to review past notifications and events captured by your cameras.
- **Customize Alert Types:**
  - Configure different types of alerts, such as motion, sound, or specific activity zones, based on your security needs.

6. Integrating with Smart Home Devices

- **Smart Home Integration:**

- If you've integrated your Arlo system with other smart home devices (e.g., Alexa, Google Assistant, or Apple HomeKit), use the app to manage these connections and create automation routines.
- **Voice Commands:**
  - Set up and manage voice commands for controlling your Arlo system through compatible smart speakers and assistants.

7. Managing Account and Subscription

- **Account Settings:**
  - Access your account settings to update your profile information, change your password, or manage account preferences.
- **Subscription Management:**
  - View and manage your subscription plans for cloud storage and additional features. Upgrade or modify your plan as needed.
- **Firmware Updates:**
  - Check for firmware updates for your Arlo devices and install them to ensure you have the latest features and security patches.

8. Troubleshooting and Support

- **Help and Support:**
  - Access the "Help" or "Support" section in the app for troubleshooting tips, FAQs, and contact information for Arlo customer support.
- **System Status:**
  - Check the system status page to view any known issues or outages affecting the Arlo network.

Live Viewing and Recording with the Arlo App

The Arlo app allows you to monitor live footage and record events from your Arlo Home Security System.

1. Live Viewing

- **Access Live Feed:**
  - ○ Open the Arlo app and log in to your account. On the home screen, you will see a list of your connected cameras.
  - ○ Tap on the camera you wish to view. The app will load the live video feed from that camera.
- **Full-Screen Mode:**
  - ○ To view the live feed in full-screen mode, tap the expand icon (usually located at the corner of the video feed). This provides a larger view and allows for easier monitoring.
- **Interacting with the Feed:**
  - ○ **Zoom In/Out:** Use pinch-to-zoom gestures on the live feed to zoom in or out. This can help you focus on specific areas or details.
  - ○ **Pan the View:** Drag your finger across the screen to pan around the live feed if your camera supports this feature.
- **Two-Way Audio:**
  - ○ If your camera has two-way audio capability, you can communicate with individuals through the camera. Tap the microphone icon to speak and the speaker icon to listen.
- **Activate or Deactivate Features:**
  - ○ While viewing the live feed, you can activate features such as night vision or motion detection by using the corresponding icons within the app.

2. Recording Video

- **Manual Recording:**
  - ○ While viewing the live feed, tap the record button (usually represented by a red circle) to start recording the video. The app will save this footage to your library.
  - ○ To stop recording, tap the record button again. The video will be automatically saved.
- **Snapshot Capture:**
  - ○ During live viewing, you can take snapshots by tapping the camera icon. The image will be saved to your device's gallery or the Arlo library.
- **Automatic Recording:**

- o Configure automatic recording settings in the device's settings menu within the app. This includes setting up motion detection or sound detection triggers for automatic recording.
- **Accessing Recorded Footage:**
  - o Navigate to the "Library" tab in the app to access recorded footage. You can view, download, or delete recordings from this section.
- **Adjust Recording Settings:**
  - o Customize recording settings such as duration, resolution, and activity zones in the camera's settings menu. This helps tailor recordings to your preferences and storage needs.

3. Managing Storage

- **Cloud Storage:**
  - o If subscribed to a cloud storage plan, your recordings will be stored in the cloud. Access these recordings via the "Library" tab. Cloud storage allows for remote access and longer retention of footage.
- **Local Storage:**
  - o Some Arlo cameras support local storage via USB drives or microSD cards. Ensure the storage device is properly connected to your base station or SmartHub.
  - o Access local storage settings through the app to manage and view recordings stored locally.
- **Managing Storage Space:**
  - o Regularly review and manage your storage to avoid running out of space. Delete unnecessary recordings and snapshots to free up space for new footage.

4. Viewing Historical Footage

- **Timeline Navigation:**
  - o Use the timeline feature in the "Library" tab to navigate through recorded footage. This allows you to quickly locate specific events or time periods.
- **Event Playback:**
  - o Tap on an event or recording to view it. You can fast-forward, rewind, or pause the footage as needed.

Note: Ensure your camera and base station are connected to a stable internet connection. Check for any network issues or disruptions. Make sure the Arlo app is updated to the latest version to ensure compatibility and access to new features. Verify that the camera settings are configured correctly for live viewing and recording. Adjust motion detection and recording schedules as needed.

Motion Detection and Alerts with the Arlo System

Motion detection and alerts are critical features of the Arlo Home Security System, designed to keep you informed of activity around your property.

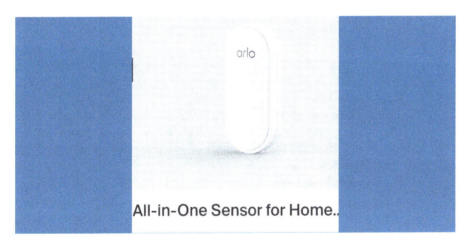

All-in-One Sensor for Home..

1. Setting Up Motion Detection

- **Access Camera Settings:**
  - o Open the Arlo app and navigate to the camera you wish to configure. Tap on the camera's name or the gear icon to access its settings.
- **Enable Motion Detection:**
  - o Ensure that motion detection is enabled. Look for the "Motion Detection" option and toggle it on if it's not already activated.
- **Adjust Sensitivity:**
  - o Customize the motion detection sensitivity to suit your needs. Lower sensitivity settings may reduce false alerts from small

movements, while higher settings increase detection range. Find the sensitivity slider in the motion detection settings and adjust it accordingly.

- **Set Up Motion Zones:**
    - o Configure specific motion detection zones to focus on areas of interest. This helps minimize notifications from less relevant areas.
    - o Use the app's interface to draw and adjust zones within the camera's field of view. Save these settings to apply them.

2. Configuring Alerts and Notifications

- **Set Up Notifications:**
    - o Go to the "Settings" menu in the Arlo app and select "Notifications." Configure how you want to receive alerts, such as push notifications, email alerts, or both.
- **Customize Alert Types:**
    - o You can choose from different alert types based on motion detection, sound detection, or specific activity zones. Enable or disable these options to tailor notifications to your preferences.
- **Set Alert Schedules:**
    - o If you only want to receive notifications during certain times, configure alert schedules. This can be useful for managing alerts during work hours or when you're asleep.

3. Using Motion Detection for Recording

- **Automatic Recording:**
    - o Configure your cameras to start recording automatically when motion is detected. This setting is found under the camera's motion detection settings.
    - o Choose the recording duration or video length to determine how long the camera will record after detecting motion.
- **Review Recorded Events:**
    - o Access recorded events triggered by motion detection in the "Library" tab of the app. Here you can review, download, or delete recordings as needed.

4. Fine-Tuning Motion Detection

- **Adjust Motion Detection Zones:**
    - o Refine motion detection zones to exclude areas with frequent movement that might cause false alarms, such as moving trees or passing cars.
- **Test and Adjust Sensitivity:**
    - o Periodically test and adjust the motion detection sensitivity based on the frequency of alerts and the environment's changing conditions.
- **Use Activity Zones:**
    - o Set up activity zones to focus the camera's motion detection on specific areas. This helps reduce unnecessary notifications from areas outside these zones.

Note: Ensure the camera is positioned correctly and is not obstructed. Adjust the camera angle and placement if necessary. Confirm that the camera and base station are connected to a stable internet connection. Poor connectivity can affect motion detection and alert delivery. Keep your Arlo devices and app updated to the latest versions to ensure optimal performance and access to new features. Double-check motion detection and alert settings to ensure they are configured as desired. Adjust settings if you're receiving too many or too few alerts.

6. Integration with Other Smart Devices

- **Smart Home Integration:**
    - o Integrate your Arlo system with other smart home devices to enhance functionality. For example, link with smart lights to automatically turn on lights when motion is detected.
- **Voice Assistants:**
    - o Use voice commands to manage motion detection settings and alerts if your Arlo system is compatible with voice assistants like Amazon Alexa or Google Assistant.

Two-Way Audio and Communication

Two-way audio allows for real-time communication through your Arlo cameras, offering enhanced interaction and control over your home security.

This feature is particularly useful for speaking with visitors, deterring intruders, or checking in on family members. Here's how to effectively use and manage two-way audio with your Arlo system:

Enabling Two-Way Audio

- **Check Camera Compatibility:**
  - o Ensure your Arlo camera model supports two-way audio. Most Arlo cameras, such as the Arlo Pro and Arlo Ultra series, include this feature.
- **Access Camera Settings:**
  - o Open the Arlo app and select the camera you want to use for two-way audio. Tap on the camera's name or gear icon to access its settings.
- **Enable Two-Way Audio:**
  - o In the camera settings, locate the option for two-way audio. Ensure it is turned on. This setting may be found under "Audio Settings" or a similar menu.

Using Two-Way Audio

- **Start a Conversation:**
  - o From the live feed view in the Arlo app, tap the microphone icon to speak through the camera. Hold the icon while speaking. Release it when you're done to stop transmitting audio.
- **Listening:**
  - o To listen to audio from the camera, tap the speaker icon in the live feed view. You'll hear the sound picked up by the camera's microphone.
- **Volume Control:**
  - o Adjust the volume settings on your device to ensure clear communication. Some cameras allow you to control the volume of the audio directly through the app.

- **Communicating with Visitors:**
  - o Use two-way audio to greet or provide instructions to visitors at your door. This can be especially useful for deliveries or managing unexpected guests.

- **Deterring Intruders:**
  - Use the feature to warn or deter intruders by speaking through the camera. Hearing a voice may discourage unwanted activity and alert intruders that they are being watched.
- **Checking on Family:**
  - Use two-way audio to communicate with family members, such as children or elderly relatives, when you're away from home.

Managing Two-Way Audio Settings

- **Adjust Audio Quality:**
  - In the app settings, you can often adjust audio quality and settings to improve communication clarity. Check for options like echo cancellation or noise reduction.
- **Privacy Settings:**
  - Ensure your privacy settings are configured appropriately. Only authorized users should have access to two-way audio features.
- **Notifications:**
  - Configure notifications related to two-way audio interactions, such as alerts when someone initiates a conversation through the camera.

If you experience poor audio quality, check the camera's placement and ensure it's not obstructed by objects that could affect sound transmission. Ensure that the camera and your mobile device are connected to a stable internet connection. Connectivity issues can affect the performance of two-way audio. Keep the Arlo app and camera firmware updated to ensure the latest features and improvements for two-way audio functionality. If you encounter persistent issues, try resetting the camera to its factory settings and reconfiguring it through the app. Protect your Arlo account with a strong password and enable two-factor authentication to prevent unauthorized access to two-way audio features. Be mindful of privacy when using two-way audio. Avoid communicating in sensitive areas where others might inadvertently overhear.

Chapter 3: Advanced Features and Settings

Arlo Smart Plans

Arlo Smart Plans enhance the functionality of your Arlo Home Security System by offering additional features and expanded capabilities. Here's an overview of the different Arlo Smart Plans and what they offer:

Arlo Safe Family Plan + Two...

1. Arlo Smart Plan Options

- **Arlo Secure Basic (Free):**
  - **Video Storage:** 30 days of cloud storage for video recordings.
  - **Live Streaming:** Access to live video feeds from your cameras.
  - **Motion and Sound Detection Alerts:** Basic motion and sound alerts.
  - **24/7 Support:** Access to Arlo's customer support.
- **Arlo Secure Plus:**
  - **Video Storage:** 60 days of cloud storage for video recordings.
  - **Live Streaming:** Access to live video feeds.
  - **Advanced Detection:** Enhanced motion and sound detection with smarter alerts.
  - **Activity Zones:** Ability to create custom activity zones for more precise alerts.

- o **Video Review:** Advanced video review features, including object detection.
- o **24/7 Support:** Priority customer support and faster response times.
- **Arlo Secure Pro:**
  - o **Video Storage:** 365 days of cloud storage for video recordings.
  - o **Live Streaming:** Access to live video feeds.
  - o **Advanced Detection:** Includes person, vehicle, and package detection.
  - o **Activity Zones:** Advanced customization for activity zones.
  - o **Video Review:** Comprehensive review options and enhanced search capabilities.
  - o **24/7 Support:** Priority support and exclusive customer service benefits.

2. Key Features of Arlo Smart Plans

- **Cloud Storage:**
  - o **Secure Basic:** 30 days of cloud storage.
  - o **Secure Plus:** 60 days of cloud storage.
  - o **Secure Pro:** 365 days of cloud storage.
- **Enhanced Detection and Alerts:**
  - o **Arlo Secure Plus & Pro:** Advanced detection capabilities including person, vehicle, and package detection. Customizable activity zones for targeted alerts.
- **Video Quality:**
  - o **Secure Plus & Pro:** Higher resolution video quality and enhanced features for clearer and more detailed footage.
- **Video Review and Search:**
  - o **Arlo Secure Pro:** Advanced video review tools, including the ability to search for specific events or objects within recordings.
- **Customer Support:**
  - o **Secure Plus & Pro:** Priority support with faster response times and access to dedicated customer service representatives.

3. Managing Your Arlo Smart Plan

- o **Upgrade or Downgrade Plans:** Easily upgrade or downgrade your plan through the Arlo app or website based on your needs.
- o **Cancel Subscription:** Manage your subscription settings and cancel if necessary through your account settings.
- o **Update Payment Information:** Keep your payment details up to date to ensure uninterrupted access to your plan features.
- o **Billing History:** View your billing history and track your subscription payments.
- o **Free Trials:** New users may be eligible for a free trial of Arlo Smart Plans. Check for trial offers when setting up your account or through promotional emails.

If you experience issues with your subscription or plan features, contact Arlo support for assistance. Ensure your plan is active and correctly applied to your account to access all included features.

Benefits of Arlo Smart Plans

- **Enhanced Security:** Additional features provide a more comprehensive security solution.
- **Improved Detection:** Smarter detection and alerts help you stay informed of important events.
- **Increased Storage:** More cloud storage means you can retain and review more footage.
- **Priority Support:** Faster and more responsive customer support ensures any issues are resolved quickly.

Integrating with Smart Home Systems

Integrating your Arlo Home Security System with other smart home systems can enhance its functionality and create a more cohesive home automation experience.

1. Integration with Amazon Alexa

- **Setup:**
    - o Open the Amazon Alexa app on your smartphone.

- o Go to the "Skills & Games" section and search for "Arlo."
- o Enable the Arlo skill and log in to your Arlo account to link it with Alexa.
- **Voice Commands:**
  - o Use voice commands to interact with your Arlo cameras, such as "Alexa, show me the front door camera" or "Alexa, record from the living room camera."
- **Routines:**
  - o Create routines that include Arlo's actions, such as turning on lights or activating the camera when a motion sensor is triggered.

2. Integration with Google Assistant

- **Setup:**
  - o Open the Google Home app on your smartphone.
  - o Tap on the "+" icon to add a new device, then select "Set up device."
  - o Search for "Arlo" and follow the prompts to link your Arlo account with Google Assistant.
- **Voice Commands:**
  - o Use voice commands to control your Arlo cameras, like "Hey Google, show me the backyard camera" or "Hey Google, turn on the security lights."
- **Automation:**
  - o Incorporate Arlo devices into Google Assistant routines, such as enabling or disabling cameras based on specific triggers or times.

3. Integration with Apple HomeKit

- **Setup:**
  - o Ensure your Arlo cameras are compatible with Apple HomeKit (e.g., Arlo Pro 3 or Arlo Ultra).
  - o Open the Home app on your iOS device.
  - o Tap the "+" icon to add a new accessory and scan the HomeKit setup code found in the Arlo app or on the camera.
- **Voice Commands:**

- o Use Siri to control your Arlo cameras with commands like "Hey Siri, show the front door camera" or "Hey Siri, turn off the camera in the living room."
- **Scenes and Automations:**
  - o Create scenes or automations that include Arlo devices, such as setting up a "Goodnight" scene that activates cameras and locks doors.

4. Integration with IFTTT (If This Then That)

- **Setup:**
  - o Open the IFTTT app or website and create an account if you don't already have one.
  - o Search for "Arlo" and connect your Arlo account with IFTTT.
- **Creating Applets:**
  - o Set up applets to automate actions between Arlo and other smart home devices. For example, you can create an applet to turn on lights when motion is detected or send alerts to your phone.
- **Custom Triggers:**
  - o Use IFTTT to create custom triggers and actions based on events detected by your Arlo cameras.

5. Integration with Smart Home Hubs

- **Setup:**
  - o If using a smart home hub like SmartThings, open the hub's app and add a new device.
  - o Search for Arlo and follow the prompts to link your Arlo account with the hub.
- **Automation:**
  - o Create automation routines that include Arlo cameras, such as setting up actions triggered by motion detection or other events.
- **Device Control:**
  - o Control Arlo devices through the hub's app, integrating them with other smart home devices for a unified control experience.

6. Benefits of Smart Home Integration

Enhanced Automation: Integrate Arlo with other smart devices to create automated responses to events, improving security and convenience.

Convenient Control: Use voice commands or app controls to manage your Arlo system along with other smart home devices.

Seamless Operation: Coordinate actions between Arlo cameras and other smart devices, such as lights and alarms, for a cohesive home security solution.

Ensure all devices are connected to the same network and that there are no connectivity issues affecting the integration. Verify that your Arlo account is properly linked to the smart home system or voice assistant. Re-link accounts if necessary.

Customizing Camera Settings in the Arlo System

Customizing your Arlo camera settings allows you to tailor the system to your specific needs, enhancing both functionality and security. Here's a detailed guide on how to adjust various camera settings through the Arlo app:

1. Accessing Camera Settings

- **Open the Arlo App:**
    - Launch the Arlo app on your smartphone or tablet.
    - Log in to your account if prompted.
- **Select the Camera:**
    - From the home screen, tap on the camera you want to configure.
    - Tap the gear icon or "Settings" to access the camera's settings menu.

2. Video Quality and Resolution

- **Adjust Resolution:**
    - In the camera settings menu, find the option for video quality or resolution.

- o Choose the resolution that suits your needs, such as HD (720p) or Full HD (1080p). Higher resolutions provide clearer video but may use more storage.
- **Optimize for Bandwidth:**
  - o If you experience bandwidth issues, consider lowering the resolution to reduce data usage and improve streaming performance.

3. Motion Detection Settings

- **Enable/Disable Motion Detection:**
  - o Toggle motion detection on or off based on your preferences.
- **Adjust Sensitivity:**
  - o Use the sensitivity slider to increase or decrease how responsive the camera is to motion. Higher sensitivity detects smaller movements but may increase false alerts.
- **Create Activity Zones:**
  - o Set up specific areas within the camera's view to focus on. This helps avoid unnecessary alerts from areas with frequent movement, like busy streets or trees.
- **Configure Detection Schedules:**
  - o Set specific times when motion detection should be active or inactive, such as during night hours or while you're away.

4. Night Vision Settings

- **Enable/Disable Night Vision:**
  - o Toggle night vision on or off. Most cameras have automatic night vision that activates in low-light conditions.
- **Adjust Infrared Settings:**
  - o Some cameras allow you to adjust the intensity of infrared lighting for improved visibility at night.

5. Audio Settings

- **Enable/Disable Audio:**
  - o Toggle the audio feature on or off depending on whether you want to hear sounds from the camera's environment.

- **Adjust Microphone Sensitivity:**
  - o If applicable, adjust the microphone sensitivity to control how much sound is picked up by the camera.

6. Recording and Storage Settings

- **Set Recording Modes:**
  - o Choose between continuous recording, scheduled recording, or recording triggered by motion or sound.
- **Manage Storage:**
  - o Configure cloud storage settings or local storage options. Ensure you have adequate storage space based on your recording needs.
- **Review and Delete Footage:**
  - o Regularly review and manage recorded footage to free up space and keep your library organized.

6. Notification Settings

- **Configure Alerts:**
  - o Set up notifications for different events, such as motion detection, sound detection, or camera tampering.
- **Adjust Alert Types:**
  - o Choose how you receive notifications, such as push notifications, email alerts, or text messages.
- **Set Up Do Not Disturb:**
  - o Create schedules to disable notifications during specific times, like while you're sleeping.

8. Power and Battery Management

- **Check Battery Status:**
  - o Monitor battery levels and receive alerts when battery power is low.
- **Optimize Battery Life:**
  - o Adjust settings such as motion detection sensitivity and video recording schedules to conserve battery life.
- **Update Power Settings:**

- o If using rechargeable batteries, manage charging schedules and battery replacements as needed.

Note: If settings issues arise, consider resetting the camera to its factory settings and reconfiguring it through the app. Ensure the camera is connected to a stable internet connection to maintain proper functionality and access to settings. Verify that the app has the necessary permissions on your device to access and manage camera settings.

Cloud Storage and Local Storage

When using Arlo cameras, you have options for storing recorded footage, each with its own advantages. Here's a comprehensive guide to understanding and managing cloud storage and local storage options for your Arlo system:

1. Cloud Storage

Overview: Cloud storage allows you to save video footage online, which you can access from anywhere with an internet connection. Arlo offers various cloud storage plans depending on your subscription.

Benefits:

- **Remote Access:** Access recorded footage from anywhere via the Arlo app or web portal.
- **Automatic Backup:** Video footage is automatically uploaded and stored securely in the cloud.
- **No Local Hardware Required:** No need for additional storage devices or physical media.
- **Easy Sharing:** Share video links or footage with others directly from the app.

Plans:

- **Arlo Secure Basic:** 30 days of cloud storage.
- **Arlo Secure Plus:** 60 days of cloud storage.
- **Arlo Secure Pro:** 365 days of cloud storage.

Managing Cloud Storage:

- **Accessing Footage:** View and manage your recordings through the Arlo app or web portal.
- **Subscription Management:** Upgrade or downgrade your plan as needed through the Arlo app.
- **Review and Delete:** Regularly review stored footage and delete old or unnecessary videos to manage storage limits.

Considerations:

- **Subscription Costs:** Cloud storage plans come with monthly or annual subscription fees.
- **Data Privacy:** Ensure your account has strong security settings to protect stored footage.

2. Local Storage

Overview: Local storage involves saving video footage on a physical device connected to your Arlo base station, such as a USB drive or a microSD card (for compatible models).

Benefits:

- **No Ongoing Fees:** Local storage doesn't require a subscription fee, as you're using your own storage media.
- **Immediate Access:** Footage is available immediately on the local storage device connected to your base station.
- **Backup Option:** Provides an additional layer of storage in case of cloud storage issues or subscription lapses.

Setting Up Local Storage:

- **Insert Storage Media:**
  - **USB Drive:** Plug a USB drive into the USB port on your Arlo base station.
  - **microSD Card:** Insert a microSD card into the base station (for compatible models).

- **Format the Drive:**
  - ○ Format the storage media if prompted by the Arlo app or base station to ensure compatibility.
- **Configure Settings:**
  - ○ Access the Arlo app and go to the settings for your base station.
  - ○ Enable local storage and configure settings for recording and overwriting.

Managing Local Storage:

- **Accessing Footage:**
  - ○ Retrieve footage directly from the connected storage media.
- **Storage Capacity:**
  - ○ Monitor the storage capacity of the connected device. Local storage devices have limited space compared to cloud options.
- **Backup and Maintenance:**
  - ○ Periodically back up important footage and check the health of your storage media.

Considerations:

- **Physical Security:** Ensure the local storage device is secure and not easily accessible to prevent tampering or theft.
- **Storage Capacity:** Manage the available space and regularly check for full or near-full storage to avoid overwriting important footage.

3. Choosing Between Cloud and Local Storage

Cloud Storage:

- Ideal for those who prefer remote access and don't want to manage physical storage devices.
- Best for users who need extended storage duration and easy sharing options.

Local Storage:

- Suitable for those looking to avoid ongoing subscription fees and prefer to keep data physically secure.
- Useful as a supplementary backup option alongside cloud storage.

Cloud Storage Issues:

- **Check Subscription Status:** Ensure your subscription is active and payments are up-to-date.
- **Verify Connectivity:** Ensure your Arlo cameras and base station have a stable internet connection.
- **Review Storage Limits:** Check if you've exceeded your storage limit and manage old footage accordingly.

Local Storage Issues:

- **Check Device Connection:** Ensure the storage media is properly connected to the base station.
- **Format Device:** Reformat the storage media if it's not recognized or if there are errors.
- **Monitor Capacity:** Regularly check the available space and manage recorded footage to prevent data loss.

Chapter 4: Troubleshooting and Support
Common Issues and Solutions for Arlo Cameras

While Arlo cameras are generally reliable, users may occasionally encounter issues. Here are some common problems and their solutions:

1. Camera Not Connecting to Wi-Fi

Symptoms:

- The camera fails to connect to the Wi-Fi network.
- "Offline" status in the Arlo app.

Check Network Status: Ensure your Wi-Fi network is working and other devices are connected.

Restart Camera and Router: Power cycle your camera by removing and reinserting the battery or unplugging it. Restart your router to refresh the network.

Reconfigure Wi-Fi Settings: Go to the Arlo app and follow the steps to reconnect the camera to your Wi-Fi network.

Check Signal Strength: Ensure the camera is within range of your router. If the signal is weak, consider moving the camera closer to the router or using a Wi-Fi extender.

2. Poor Video Quality or Lag

Symptoms:

- The video appears blurry or pixelated.
- Lag or delays in live streaming.

Adjust Resolution Settings: In the Arlo app, adjust the video resolution to a lower setting if the quality is too high for your network bandwidth.

Improve Network Speed: Ensure you have a stable and fast internet connection. Consider upgrading your router or network plan if necessary.

Check Camera Placement: Ensure the camera is not obstructed and has a clear view. Reduce interference from other electronic devices.

3. Motion Detection Issues

Symptoms:

- Motion detection alerts are not received.
- The camera fails to record motion events.

Verify Sensitivity Settings: Adjust the motion detection sensitivity in the Arlo app to ensure it's appropriately set for your needs.

Configure Activity Zones: Check and update your activity zones to ensure important areas are monitored and minimize false alerts.

Check Firmware Updates: Ensure your camera firmware is up-to-date to benefit from the latest improvements and bug fixes.

4. Battery Draining Quickly

Symptoms: Camera batteries deplete faster than expected.

Check Battery Usage: Monitor battery levels in the Arlo app and replace batteries as needed. Consider using high-quality batteries for longer life.

Optimize Camera Settings: Reduce motion detection sensitivity or adjust recording schedules to minimize battery consumption.

Check for Interference: Ensure the camera is not placed near devices or in locations that cause high battery drain due to constant connectivity issues.

5. No Sound or Audio Issues

Symptoms:

- No audio is heard through the camera.
- Issues with two-way audio functionality.

Check Audio Settings: Ensure audio settings are enabled in the Arlo app. Verify that the microphone and speaker are working properly.

Restart Camera: Restart the camera to reset its audio components.

Check Network Connection: Ensure you have a stable internet connection, as poor connectivity can affect audio performance.

6. Issues with Arlo App

Symptoms:

- The app crashes or fails to load.
- Features not working as expected.

Update the App: Ensure you have the latest version of the Arlo app installed. Update it through the App Store or Google Play Store.

Clear Cache and Data: Clear the app's cache and data from your device settings if the app is slow or unresponsive.

Reinstall the App: Uninstall and reinstall the Arlo app to resolve persistent issues.

7. Local Storage Problems

Symptoms: Issues with accessing or recording to local storage.

Check Storage Media: Ensure the USB drive or microSD card is properly inserted into the base station and is formatted correctly.

Verify Capacity: Check the storage media's capacity and free up space if necessary.

Format Device: Reformat the storage media if it's not recognized by the base station or if there are errors.

8. Cloud Storage Issues

Symptoms:

- Issues with accessing cloud recordings.
- Notifications about storage limits or subscription problems.

Verify Subscription Status: Ensure your cloud storage subscription is active and payments are up-to-date.

Check Connectivity: Ensure your camera and base station have a stable internet connection for proper cloud upload.

Review Storage Settings: Regularly review and manage stored footage through the Arlo app to stay within your storage limits.

9. Firmware Update Problems

Symptoms: Issues with installing firmware updates.

Check for Updates: Ensure your camera and base station are running the latest firmware. Check for updates in the Arlo app.

Restart Devices: Restart your camera and base station to ensure they are ready for the update.

Manual Update: If automatic updates fail, check the Arlo support website for manual update instructions.

Firmware Updates for Arlo Cameras

Firmware updates are essential for maintaining the performance, of your Arlo cameras. They provide new features, improve existing ones, and fix bugs.

1. Purpose of Firmware Updates

- **Enhance Features:** Add new functionalities or improve existing features.
- **Improve Security:** Fix vulnerabilities and improve overall security.
- **Fix Bugs:** Resolve known issues and improve system stability.
- **Optimize Performance:** Enhance the efficiency and reliability of your cameras.

2. Checking for Firmware Updates

Via the Arlo App:

- o **Open the Arlo App:** Launch the Arlo app on your smartphone or tablet.
- **Go to Device Settings:**
  - o Tap on the camera or base station you want to check.
  - o Go to "Settings" and select "Device Info" or "Firmware."
  - o **Check for Updates:** The app will display if a firmware update is available. Follow prompts to start the update process if necessary.

Via the Arlo Web Portal:

- o **Log In:** Access the Arlo web portal at arlo.com and log in to your account.
- o **Navigate to Devices:** Select the camera or base station from the list of devices.
- o **Check Firmware Version:** View the current firmware version and check if an update is available. Follow on-screen instructions to update.

3. Updating Firmware

Automatic Updates:

- o **Default Setting:** Arlo cameras are typically set to update firmware automatically. Ensure your device is connected to the internet to receive updates.
- o **Monitoring:** Regularly check the app or web portal to ensure updates are applied.

Manual Updates:

- o **Initiate Update:** If automatic updates are disabled or you prefer to update manually, follow the instructions provided in the app or web portal.
- o **Download and Install:** The app or portal will guide you through downloading and installing the firmware update. Ensure your camera is connected to power and the internet during the update.

Verify Functionality:

- o **Check Device Performance:** Test the camera to ensure it's operating correctly after the update.
- o **Review Settings:** Confirm that your settings and configurations are intact and functioning as expected.

Monitor for Issues:

- o **Watch for Bugs:** Keep an eye out for any new issues or performance changes after the update and report them if necessary.
- o **Update Regularly:** Regularly check for firmware updates to keep your system secure and up-to-date.

Best Practices for Firmware Updates

- o **Ensure Power Supply:** Keep your camera and base station connected to a reliable power source during updates.
- o **Stable Internet Connection:** Maintain a stable internet connection to facilitate smooth updates.
- o **Regular Updates:** Regularly check for and apply firmware updates to benefit from new features and improvements.

Resetting Your Arlo System

Resetting your Arlo system can resolve various issues, such as connectivity problems, malfunctioning devices, or when you need to start from scratch. There are different types of resets you can perform, depending on whether you need to reset an individual camera or the entire system.

Factory Reset:

- o **Locate the Reset Button:** Find the reset button on your Arlo camera. This is typically a small, pinhole-sized button that requires a paperclip or similar tool to press.

- o **Press and Hold:** Use a paperclip to press and hold the reset button for about 10 seconds. The camera's LED will blink to indicate that the reset process has started.
- o **Release and Wait:** Release the button when the LED starts flashing rapidly, indicating that the camera is resetting. Wait for the camera to reboot, which may take a few minutes.
- o **Reconfigure the Camera:** After the reset, you'll need to set up the camera again through the Arlo app or web portal, including reconnecting to your Wi-Fi network and reconfiguring settings.

Soft Reset (Power Cycle):

- o **Remove Power Source:** For battery-powered cameras, remove the battery. For wired cameras, unplug the power adapter.
- o **Wait and Reinsert:** Wait for about 10 seconds and then reinsert the battery or plug in the power adapter.
- o **Restart Camera:** Wait for the camera to reboot and reconnect to the network.

Resetting the Arlo Base Station

Factory Reset:

- o **Locate the Reset Button:** Find the reset button on your Arlo base station. This is usually a small, pinhole-sized button that requires a paperclip or similar tool.
- o **Press and Hold:** Use a paperclip to press and hold the reset button for about 10 seconds. The base station's LED will blink to indicate that the reset process is in progress.
- o **Release and Wait:** Release the button when the LED starts flashing rapidly. Wait for the base station to reboot and complete the reset process, which may take several minutes.
- o **Reconfigure the Base Station:** After the reset, you will need to set up the base station again through the Arlo app or web portal, including reconnecting it to your Wi-Fi network and adding cameras back to the system.

Soft Reset (Power Cycle):

- o **Unplug and Wait:** Unplug the base station from the power source and wait for about 10 seconds.
- o **Reconnect Power:** Plug the base station back into the power source and wait for it to restart and reconnect to the network.

. Resetting the Arlo System

Complete System Reset:

- o **Reset Base Station:** Perform a factory reset on the base station as described above. This will remove all paired cameras and reset the base station to factory settings.
- o **Remove and Re-add Cameras:** After resetting the base station, you will need to remove all cameras from the system and then re-add them one by one through the Arlo app or web portal.
- o **Reconfigure System Settings:** Set up your Arlo system again, including Wi-Fi network settings, motion detection zones, and recording schedules.

Important Considerations:

- o **Backup Settings:** If possible, note your current settings or configurations before performing a reset to ease the reconfiguration process.
- o **Firmware Updates:** After resetting, check for and apply any available firmware updates to ensure your devices are running the latest software

Note: Ensure that your camera and base station are within range of your Wi-Fi network and that the network is working properly. Verify that all devices have the latest firmware updates installed. If issues persist after resetting, contact Arlo customer support for further assistance.

Contacting Arlo Support

If you encounter issues with your Arlo system that you cannot resolve through troubleshooting or resetting, contacting Arlo support can provide you with expert assistance.

1. Gathering Information Before Contacting Support

Before reaching out, gather the following information to expedite the support process:

- o **Account Information:** Your Arlo account email address and any associated account details.
- o **Device Information:** Model numbers and serial numbers of the Arlo cameras and base station.
- o **Firmware Version:** The current firmware version of your devices can be found in the device settings within the Arlo app or web portal.
- o **Issue Details:** A clear description of the problem you are experiencing, including any error messages or specific symptoms.
- o **Troubleshooting Steps Taken:** Document any troubleshooting steps you have already attempted.

2. Contacting Via the Arlo App:

- o **Open the App:** Launch the Arlo app on your smartphone or tablet.
- o **Access Support:** Go to the menu and select "Support" or "Help."
- o **Submit a Request:** Follow the prompts to submit a support request or chat with a support agent.

Via the Arlo Web Portal:

- o **Log In:** Go to the Arlo web portal and log in to your account.
- o **Visit Support Center:** Navigate to the "Support" section from the menu.
- o **Contact Support:** Choose the method to contact support, such as live chat, email, or submitting a support ticket.

Via Phone:

- **Find the Number:** Look up the support phone number for your region on the Arlo support website. Arlo support typically offers phone support in various countries.
- **Call Support:** Call the number provided and follow the prompts to speak with a support representative.

Via Email:

- **Email Support:** Send an email to the support address listed on the Arlo support website or within the app. Include all relevant information and a detailed description of your issue.

Support Resources:

- **Arlo Support Website:** Visit the Arlo Support Center for FAQs, troubleshooting guides, and other resources.
- **Community Forums:** Check the Arlo Community Forums for advice and solutions from other users.

3. Following Up

- **Track Your Request:** If you've submitted a support ticket, keep track of any reference numbers or communication threads.
- **Provide Additional Information:** Respond promptly to any requests for additional information from Arlo support.
- **Evaluate Solutions:** Once you receive a solution or guidance, evaluate it to ensure the issue is resolved satisfactorily.

4. Tips for Effective Support Communication

- **Be Clear and Concise:** Clearly describe your issue and any troubleshooting steps taken to avoid unnecessary back-and-forth.

- Be Patient: Support teams may need time to investigate and resolve complex issues. Allow time for responses and follow-up.
- Provide Feedback: After your issue is resolved, provide feedback on your support experience to help improve service quality.

Chapter 5: Maintenance and Care

Regular maintenance of your Arlo cameras and equipment ensures optimal performance and longevity. Proper care helps prevent issues and keeps your security system functioning effectively.

Cleaning Your Cameras

Exterior Cleaning:

- **Use a Soft Cloth:** Gently wipe the camera's exterior with a microfiber cloth to remove dust and dirt. Avoid abrasive materials that could scratch the surface.
- **Avoid Moisture:** Do not use water or cleaning solutions directly on the camera. Instead, lightly dampen the cloth if necessary.
- **Check Lenses:** Clean the camera lens with a lens-cleaning cloth to ensure clear video footage. Be gentle to avoid scratching the lens.

Interior Cleaning:

- **Battery Contacts:** For battery-powered models, occasionally clean the battery contacts with a dry cloth to ensure good electrical connections.

Battery Maintenance

Battery Replacement:

- **Monitor Battery Levels:** Regularly check the battery levels in the Arlo app or web portal and replace batteries when they are low.
- **Use High-Quality Batteries:** Use high-quality, recommended batteries to ensure longer life and better performance.

Battery Storage:

- o **Store Properly:** If storing spare batteries, keep them in a cool, dry place. Avoid exposing them to extreme temperatures or moisture.

. Checking Camera Placement

Optimal Positioning:

- o **Adjust Angles:** Regularly check and adjust camera angles to ensure optimal coverage and avoid obstructions.
- o **Secure Mounting:** Ensure cameras are securely mounted and not subject to movement or tampering.

Environmental Conditions:

- o **Protect from Elements:** If cameras are placed outdoors, ensure they are protected from harsh weather conditions. Use weather-resistant covers if necessary.
- o **Avoid Direct Sunlight:** Position cameras to minimize exposure to direct sunlight, which can affect video quality and damage the camera.

Managing Storage

Cloud Storage:

- o **Monitor Usage:** Regularly review and manage cloud storage to stay within your subscription limits.
- o **Manage Recordings:** Delete old or unnecessary recordings to free up space and ensure important footage is retained.

Local Storage:

- o **Check Storage Media:** Regularly check and manage the storage media (USB drive or microSD card) connected to your base station.
- o **Format as Needed:** Reformat storage media if it becomes corrupted or if the base station prompts for a format.

System Health Checks

Connectivity:

- o **Verify Network Connection:** Ensure your cameras and base station are connected to a stable Wi-Fi network. Address any connectivity issues promptly.
- o **Test Functionality:** Periodically test all system functions, including live viewing, motion detection, and recording.

If you notice any issues with your cameras or system performance, follow the troubleshooting steps or contact Arlo support for assistance.

. Security Measures

Account Security:

- o **Use Strong Passwords:** Ensure your Arlo account password is strong and unique. Update it regularly and enable two-factor authentication if available.
- o **Monitor Access:** Regularly review and manage user access to your Arlo account and devices.

Physical Security:

- o **Protect Equipment:** Secure your cameras and base station to prevent tampering or theft. Use locks or enclosures if necessary.

Record Keeping

Documentation:

- o **Maintain Records:** Keep records of any maintenance tasks performed, including battery replacements, firmware updates, and cleaning schedules.

Warranty Information:

- o **Track Warranty Status:** Keep track of the warranty period for your Arlo devices and note any relevant support or service information.

Security and Privacy Best Practices

Ensuring the security and privacy of your Arlo cameras is crucial to protect your home and personal data. Follow these best practices:

1. Secure Your Arlo Account

Use Strong Passwords:

- o **Create Complex Passwords:** Use a combination of letters, numbers, and special characters for your Arlo account password.
- o **Avoid Common Passwords:** Do not use easily guessable passwords such as "password123" or personal information.

Enable Two-Factor Authentication (2FA):

- o **Add an Extra Layer:** Enable two-factor authentication for your Arlo account to add an additional layer of security. This requires a verification code in addition to your password.

Regularly Update Passwords:

- o **Change Passwords Periodically:** Regularly update your Arlo account password and ensure it is unique to your Arlo account.

2. Secure Your Network

Use a Strong Wi-Fi Password:

- o **Create a Robust Password:** Ensure your Wi-Fi network password is strong and secure to prevent unauthorized access.

Update Router Firmware:

- o **Keep Firmware Current:** Regularly update your router's firmware to protect against vulnerabilities and enhance security.

Network Segmentation:

- o **Separate Networks:** If possible, use separate networks for your IoT devices, including Arlo cameras, to limit exposure in case of a network breach.

3. Manage Camera and Device Access

Review and Control User Access:

- o **Manage User Permissions:** Regularly review and manage who has access to your Arlo system through the app or web portal. Remove access for users who no longer need it.

Use Device-Based Authentication:

- o **Secure Device Logins:** If available, use device-based authentication (such as fingerprint or face recognition) for accessing the Arlo app.

Disable Remote Access When Not Needed:

- o **Limit Access:** If you don't need remote access, disable it to reduce the risk of unauthorized access.

4. Configure Privacy Settings

Adjust Camera Settings:

- o **Manage Motion Detection:** Set appropriate motion detection zones to avoid capturing unnecessary areas and protect privacy.

- o **Control Notifications:** Configure notification settings to ensure you are alerted to important events without excessive notifications.

Disable Audio Recording:

- o **Respect Privacy:** If privacy is a concern, disable audio recording features on your cameras to ensure conversations are not recorded without consent.

Regularly Review Camera Placement:

- o **Verify Coverage:** Ensure your cameras are positioned to cover desired areas while respecting the privacy of neighbours and passersby.

5. Protect Data and Storage

Secure Cloud Storage:

- o **Manage Access:** Regularly review who has access to your cloud recordings and ensure your cloud storage account is secure.

Protect Local Storage:

- o **Secure Physical Media:** If using local storage (e.g., USB drive or microSD card), ensure it is physically secure and regularly check its integrity.

Regularly Back Up Data:

Cellular & Battery Backup

- o **Maintain Backups:** Regularly back up important footage and data to prevent loss in case of system failure or data corruption.

6. Stay Informed and Updated

Monitor Security Alerts:

- o **Stay Updated:** Stay informed about any security vulnerabilities or updates related to Arlo devices by checking the Arlo website or support portal.

Apply Firmware Updates:

- o **Update Regularly:** Regularly check for and apply firmware updates to ensure your devices have the latest security patches and improvements.

Educate Yourself on Best Practices:

- o **Stay Knowledgeable:** Stay informed about best practices for security and privacy for connected devices to maintain a secure home network.

7. Respond to Security Incidents

Report Suspicious Activity:

- ○ **Contact Support:** Report any suspicious activity or security concerns to Arlo support immediately.

Review Security Logs:

- ○ **Check Logs:** Regularly review security logs and notifications for any unusual activity or potential breaches.

Take Immediate Action:

- ○ **Address Issues Promptly:** Take immediate action to secure your system and mitigate any risks if you suspect a security breach.

Additional Resources

If you find yourself unable to locate the information you need in this user guide, don't worry—there are several additional resources available to help you out. Here's a quick overview of where you can turn for more assistance:

1. Arlo Support Center

The Arlo Support Center is a comprehensive resource that offers a wealth of information beyond what's covered in this guide. Whether you're looking for detailed troubleshooting steps, FAQs, or setup instructions, the support centre is a great place to start. You can access it directly through the Arlo website or via the Arlo app. Here, you'll find articles and guides tailored to specific issues and device models.

2. Community Forums

Sometimes, the best advice comes from fellow users who have faced similar challenges. The Arlo Community Forums are an excellent platform to engage with other Arlo users. You can browse through existing discussions, ask questions, and share your experiences. Many users and Arlo enthusiasts actively contribute to these forums, offering valuable insights and solutions.

3. Arlo Customer Support

If you're still having trouble finding a resolution, reaching out to Arlo's customer support team can be incredibly helpful. They offer support via live chat, email, and phone. When contacting support, be sure to have your device information and a detailed description of the issue ready. This will help them provide a more accurate and efficient solution.

4. Social Media and Online Resources

Arlo also maintains a presence on social media platforms like Twitter and Facebook. Sometimes, these channels provide timely updates, tips, and community interaction that might not be available in the traditional support channels. Additionally, various tech blogs and review sites offer practical advice and how-to guides that can provide further insights into using your Arlo system.

5. Product Manuals and Documentation

For in-depth technical details, refer to the product manuals and official documentation provided with your Arlo equipment. These documents often include detailed specifications, installation guides, and

Warranty and Return Information

Understanding the warranty and return policies for your Arlo system is important to ensure you can address any issues with your devices effectively.

1. Warranty Coverage

Standard Warranty:

- **Duration:**
    - Arlo typically offers a one-year limited warranty for most of their products. However, the warranty duration may vary depending on the product model and region. Check your specific product's warranty terms for precise information.
- **Coverage:**

- The warranty covers defects in materials and workmanship under normal use. It does not cover damage caused by misuse, unauthorized modifications, or accidents.

Extended Warranty:

- **Extended Plans:**
  - Arlo offers extended warranty plans for some products, which you can purchase separately. These plans may provide additional coverage beyond the standard warranty period.

Warranty Registration:

- To activate your warranty and receive updates, it's advisable to register your Arlo product on the Arlo website. This can simplify the warranty claim process if needed.

2. Warranty Claims Eligibility:

- **Check Eligibility:**
  - Ensure that your issue is covered under warranty by reviewing the warranty terms. Warranty claims are generally accepted for manufacturing defects but not for damage caused by improper use or accidents.

Claim Process:

- **Contact Arlo Support:**
  - Reach out to Arlo customer support to start the warranty claim process. Provide details about your product, including the model number, serial number, and a description of the issue.
- **Provide Proof of Purchase:**
  - You may be required to provide proof of purchase, such as a receipt or order confirmation, to validate your warranty claim.
- **Follow Instructions:**

- Follow the instructions provided by Arlo support for returning the defective product or obtaining a replacement.

Repair or Replacement:

- **Options:**
  - Depending on the nature of the issue, Arlo may offer repair, replacement, or a refund. The exact resolution will be determined based on the warranty terms and the specific problem with the product.

3. Return Policy

Return Period:

- **Standard Return Window:**
  - Arlo typically offers a 30-day return period for products purchased directly from their website or authorized retailers. Check your purchase receipt or the retailer's return policy for exact details.

Return Conditions:

- **Product Condition:**
  - To qualify for a return, the product generally needs to be in its original condition and packaging. Some retailers may also require that all accessories, manuals, and parts be included.
- **Return Authorization:**
  - Obtain a return authorization from Arlo or the retailer before sending back the product. This helps ensure the return is processed correctly and promptly.

Return Process:

- **Contact Support:**
  - Reach out to Arlo customer support or the retailer to initiate the return process. Provide necessary information, such as your order number and reason for the return.

- **Ship the Product:**
  - ○ Follow the instructions provided for shipping the product back. Ensure that you use a secure shipping method and retain proof of shipment.

Refunds:

- **Processing Time:**
  - ○ Refunds are typically processed once the returned product is received and inspected. The time it takes to receive your refund may vary based on the payment method and processing times.

4. Additional Information

International Returns:

- **Regional Policies:**
  - ○ If you purchased your Arlo product from an international retailer or are located outside of the region where you purchased the product, return and warranty policies may differ. Check with local Arlo support or the retailer for specific information.

Retailer Policies:

- **Check Retailer Terms:**
  - ○ If you purchased your Arlo product from a third-party retailer, their return and warranty policies may apply. Consult the retailer's return policy for guidance.